VISUAL TIMELINES WORLD HISTORY

FROM THE STONE AGE TO THE 21ST CENTURY

ANNE ROONEY

ILLUSTRATED BY VIOLET TOBACCO

ARCTURUS

WHO'S ON THE COVER?

These are the people, animals, and objects on the cover, and a list of pages where you can find more information about them.

1 First World War soldier, page 98
2 Roman legionary, page 40
3 Samurai warrior, page 62
4 Cleopatra, page 39
5 Oxen plow, page 12
6 Combine harvester, page 85
7 Vincent van Gogh, page 90
8 Cave painting, page 10
9 Aztec pyramid, page 65
10 Moai statues, pages 5 and 63

ARCTURUS

This edition published in 2023 by Arcturus Publishing Limited
26/27 Bickels Yard, 151–153 Bermondsey Street,
London SE1 3HA

Author: Anne Rooney
Consultants: Ian Fitzgerald and Andrea Page
Illustrator: Violet Tobacco
Designer: Tokiko Morishima
Editors: Becca Clunes and Lucy Doncaster
Design Manager: Jessica Holliland
Editorial Manager: Joe Harris

ISBN: 978-1-3988-3115-5
CH010467US
Supplier 42, Date 0823, PI 00003652

Printed in Singapore

CONTENTS

INTRODUCTION

Everything that happened before this morning is history! History is the story of the past, of all human activities through time. It covers everything from natural disasters and wars, to inventions, discoveries, and much, much more. History is more than just a string of events, though. One event can cause other things to happen—sometimes unexpectedly—and history slowly builds into patterns. How people respond to an event often determines what happens next. A basic understanding of history is vital to understanding the modern world we live in.

Before history . . .

… was prehistory! This was the period when early humans were spreading around the world, then making settlements and building communities. People began to settle and farm the land around 12,000 years ago. This has sometimes been called the "Agricultural Revolution" or the "Neolithic Revolution," and it was a turning point for humans. Farming provided a reliable supply of food, allowing the population to grow. Small settlements eventually grew into cities. People took on specialized types of work, and began to build civilizations with lasting architecture, art, and eventually writing. They began to make history.

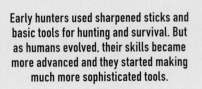

Early hunters used sharpened sticks and basic tools for hunting and survival. But as humans evolved, their skills became more advanced and they started making much more sophisticated tools.

Making history

Many historians think of history as starting around 5,000 years ago (3000 BCE). That's about the time people in some parts of the world developed ways of writing. Although written historical records are very useful to historians, they are not the only kind of historical evidence we can use. We can learn a lot from objects, art, buildings, monuments—and even from graves and dead bodies. History is put together not just by historians, but also archaeologists (who work with buildings and other human-made objects) and anthropologists (who work with evidence of human lives). If we restricted history to only studying written records, we could say nothing at all about cultures that left no writing.

Objects like the Great Sphinx of Giza reveal the skills of people who lived thousands of years ago, but we don't always know how or why they made things like this

Whose history?

When you think of history, you might think of famous individuals, such as rulers or great explorers or scientists. Or you might think of whole cultures that you know something about, such as the Romans, the ancient Chinese, or the Aztecs. You probably don't think of an Australian Indigenous person hunting kangaroo 400 years ago, a Russian serf struggling to survive on frozen farmland in the 18th century, or an Abyssinian woman weaving cloth 3,000 years ago. Most of the people who have ever lived have been ordinary people like this. But without them, the events we do know about could not have happened—they grew the food and made the tools that made everything else possible. Sometimes, we can learn about their lives even if we don't know their names.

We know nothing of the lives of the people who made these vast stone statues in Rapa Nui (Easter Island)

Most people lived ordinary lives that we only know about in general terms

5

Reading history

We know most about the cultures that have left written records that we can read. Some cultures had writing, but we haven't learned to interpret it yet. Others left no writing at all, and historians can work only from what other cultures have written about them, and from the objects they have left behind.

The Thule of Greenland left no writing, and even the Vikings who encountered them left no accounts of them

Second-hand information

Historians need to be very careful when using what one society has written about another. It's often impossible to say how accurate their accounts are, or whether they had any reason to misrepresent the people they encountered. For example, Europeans often thought of the people already living in lands they wanted to conquer as being unsophisticated, ignorant, or barbaric. They felt this excused them from stealing the land and resources of those people. When one group is at war with another, they frequently present their enemies in a bad light, sometimes making up tales of terrible things they do in order to spur on their own soldiers. It's hard to know, years later, which stories are true.

Viking raids in Europe were recorded by monks, but we don't have the Vikings' own version of what happened

Two sides to history

Even without deliberate bias, there are always at least two sides to any story. The same event reported by two people will sound different, even if they are not opponents. The same event can mean different things to different people.

One thing after another

History is as much about interpreting the events of the past as it is knowing what they were. Events have consequences, and how people feel about events has consequences. Often, it's impossible to see at the time how a situation will work out. But by knowing what has happened in the past, we can try to avoid repeating the same mistakes.

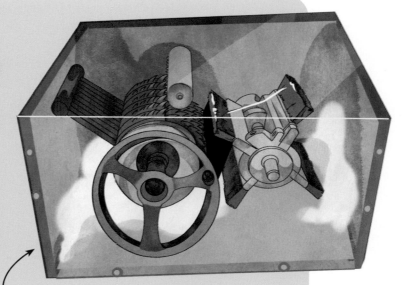

The cotton gin was invented in 1793, to make the work of producing cotton easier. It led to an increase in slavery in the USA, and so indirectly led to the American Civil War.

The random event of the Black Death in the 1340s changed the history of the world

As well as deliberate actions by people, history can be shaped by unexpected events. These range from natural disasters such as an earthquake that destroys a city, to a surprise discovery or invention that forever changes how people live. Fifty years ago, no one could have predicted that we would live much of our lives online. We don't know what will happen next, or which of the things happening now will look most important to future historians, but history is being made all the time.

CHAPTER 1

THE BEGINNING OF HISTORY

The story of world history begins with its prologue—prehistory. This time began when early modern humans spread around the world, starting in Africa, and ventured over land, and eventually sea, to start lives in all kinds of environments. They built homes from the materials available wherever they found themselves, and learned to use fire and make tools and clothes. They finally settled in fixed communities, securing their food supply by keeping animals as livestock and growing plants as crops. This was a time before people had developed written language, so what we know of them and their lives comes from objects they have left behind, including tools, works of art, shelters and other buildings, jewelry, and clothing. Even their bodies provide evidence. We can date bones to discover when people lived in the places where their remains are found, and work out what they ate and even the diseases they suffered from.

Once people began writing, recording the events and experiences of their everyday lives, history began. This started at different times around the world.

PREHISTORY—11,000 YEARS AGO (9000 BCE)

Early modern humans evolved in Africa and first left about 180,000 years ago, spreading into western Asia. Later, waves of migrating people followed. Over thousands of years, they traveled long distances to settle all around the globe. At times, sea levels allowed people to cross land bridges between areas that are now separated by water.

45,000 YEARS AGO

Mammoth-bone shelters were made in Moldova, eastern Europe. The shelters were made from piled mammoth bones covered with hides.

44,000 YEARS AGO

A notched bone and sticks from the Border cave in Africa are the first evidence of humans **counting** or **tallying** (keeping track of numbers).

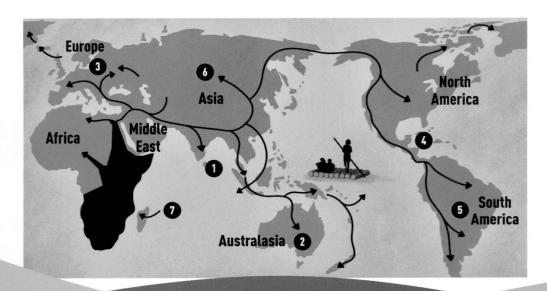

❶ 180,000 years ago
❷ 65,000 years ago
❸ 54,000 years ago
❹ 33,000 years ago
❺ 26,000 years ago
❻ 25,000 years ago
❼ 1,500 years ago

PREHISTORY

110,000–11,700 YEARS AGO

During the last glacial period (or "ice age"), sea levels fell as water was trapped as ice, revealing new **land bridges**. One was Beringia around 35,700 years ago, joining eastern Russia and the west of North America. Another later one (16,000 years ago) was Doggerland, joining Britain to continental Europe.

Ice covered much of North America, northern Russia, and Europe, while land was exposed that is now under water

54,000 YEARS AGO

Early modern humans arrived in **Europe**, joining another type of early human, **Neanderthals**, who already lived there. The two species lived alongside each other and even had families together.

50,000–45,000 YEARS AGO

The first people settled in **Australia**.

45,500 YEARS AGO

People in Indonesia **painted animals** on the walls of their caves.

A cave painting 44,000 years old is the earliest hunting scene

33,000–30,000 YEARS AGO

The first early humans probably arrived in the **Americas**.

Stone spearheads were fixed to a wooden shaft and used for hunting. Some spearheads were made from mammoth ivory.

c. 30,000 YEARS AGO

The people of Dolní Věstonice in the Czech Republic used a variety of **stone tools** for cutting, hunting, warfare, and piercing holes in leather. They also used **mammoth ivory** to make spearheads—one of the earliest known examples of this type of tool.

Agriculture changed humans, the land, and other species. People bred from the animals that gave the best meat, hide, or milk, reinforcing the characteristics they wanted. They did the same with plants, keeping seed from the best crops to grow the next year. The land was affected by people cutting down trees and clearing scrub to gain farmland, and later by them diverting water to their crops. By living close to each other and their livestock, people also became vulnerable to illness. Diseases moved from animals to people, and spread between those living in close quarters.

12,000 YEARS AGO

There was a shift from migration/hunter-gathering to settled **farming** in communities. This change happened independently at different times globally, with people settling, growing crops, and keeping animals for food. It changed human society forever.

11,000 YEARS AGO (9000 BCE)

12,500 YEARS AGO

Distinctive **"cord marked" pottery** characterized the Jōmon culture of prehistoric Japan.

29,000–15,000 YEARS AGO

Humans began to **domesticate wolves**, using them to guard animals and perhaps communities. Domesticated wolves eventually became dogs.

Wolves were probably domesticated many times, by different groups of people

9600–8200 BCE

The oldest **megaliths** (large stone monuments) were made in Göbekli Tepe, Turkey. Most (95 percent) of the site is still unexplored.

No one knows how the circle of megaliths was used

26,000 YEARS AGO

The people of Dolní Věstonice were already accomplished **artists**, and left behind figures made of ivory and clay.

8999–3500 BCE

Around 11,700 years ago (9700 BCE), the last glacial period ended. The warmer climate made farming—and life—easier. Settlements grew larger, becoming the first cities. Civilization emerged independently in six places around the world: Egypt, Mesopotamia (now Iraq and Iran), the Indus Valley (now Pakistan and Afghanistan), Mexico, Peru, and China. From here on, dates are given in the form BCE (Before Common Era) and CE (Common Era). The Common Era starts with year 1 in our current date scheme, just over 2,020 years ago. Many dates are approximate.

6000 BCE
The Sahara Desert began to **dry up**, forcing out people who lived there.

8000 BCE
One of the earliest cities, Jericho, was built from **bricks made from clay** baked in the sun.

7000 BCE
People in northeastern Siberia traded in tools made of **obsidian** (volcanic glass), apparently traveling hundreds of miles, probably by dog sled.

6000–4000 BCE
Farmers on the Greek island of Crete grew **olives**, which became a staple of trade.

8999 BCE

8000 BCE
Sea levels rose, separating the islands of Japan from mainland Asia. People who had followed herds overland and started the Jōmon culture in c. 14000 BCE were cut off. As they ran out of animals to eat, they turned to fishing, starting Japan's long tradition of fish-eating.

5000 BCE
In the Atacama desert of Chile and Peru, the Chinchorro people **mummified their dead** 2,000 years before the Egyptians began mummification.

Chinchorro bodies were taken apart, dried, then reassembled with padding of soil, ash, and grasses. They were then covered with an ash paste, and painted black.

Russia　　　　**Alaska**

8000 BCE
Beringia disappeared under the sea. **Warming weather** allowed people to settle in Canada.

With melting ice, sea levels rose, separating Russia and Alaska

■ Sea　　■ Land today　　Land 10,000 years ago

c. 6000–5000 BCE
In Mesopotamia and elsewhere, oxen were domesticated and **plows** (sometimes spelled "ploughs") for farming were developed.

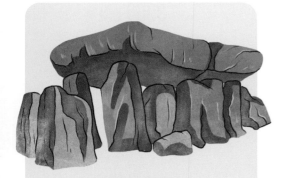

5000–4000 BCE

In France and Britain, people constructed **dolmens** (a stone slab on top of two upright stones) to bury their dead.

3500 BCE

In Mesopotamia, people built the first **ziggurats** (stepped pyramids) using mud bricks. Considered the earthly homes of gods and goddesses, these were often the first buildings in a new city.

3500 BCE

c. 4500 BCE

People in Serbia were the first to **smelt copper** to make tools.

4000 BCE

Egyptian farmers used tools to break up the soil before **sowing seeds**.

Starting in Serbia around 4500 BCE, people made bronze by mixing tin with copper. From there, the technology gradually spread to other parts of Europe and the Middle East, meaning that the Bronze Age began at different times around the world. It had a huge impact, giving people strong, lasting tools that could be made in complex shapes. This led to the development of more sophisticated agricultural practices, as well as the creation of more effective weapons for hunting and warfare. Those with bronze tools and weapons had a great advantage over groups without them. It also allowed for the creation of more complex societies with greater specialization of labor, and paved the way for further technological advances in metalworking.

3500 BCE–1000 CE

The **Bantu** people spread from the River Niger throughout most of sub-Saharan Africa. They made iron tools, which they used alongside their stone tools. This made their farming efficient. More than 500 modern African languages have developed from Bantu.

3500 BCE

The Telarmachay civilization of the Peruvian Andes kept **llamas and alpacas**, using their hair to make fabrics and eating their meat.

3499–2500 BCE

Larger settlements grew into the first cities. Individuals no longer provided everything needed for themselves and their families. Instead, tasks were shared out—some people grew or prepared food, others built homes, or served the gods. Administration and bureaucracy became essential to organize work and share the benefits.

3000 BCE

The **potter's wheel** was invented as a horizontal surface the potter turned while shaping a pot. The wheel was later adapted for transport.

3490 BCE

On the central Asian steppe, probably in Ukraine or Kazakhstan, people began to **domesticate horses**.

The first domesticated horses were small and stout

3100 BCE

The first **Egyptian dynasty** began, with the unification of southern and northern Egypt. A dynasty is a period when rulers come from the same family line.

3000 BCE

In Mesopotamia, the **shadoof** was used to lift water in a bucket from a river, pool, or well. A heavy counterweight lifted the filled bucket. With a shadoof, people could water their crops more easily, since the work of lifting was done by the lever, not the farmworker.

3499 BCE

3100–2800 BCE

Sumer (in modern Iraq) rose in power. It remained one of the most important regions for thousands of years.

The Indus Valley civilization in Pakistan, Afghanistan, and India began around 3300 BCE. An extremely sophisticated civilization, it had advanced building and town planning, with good plumbing (including flushing toilets) and roads set out on a grid pattern. The largest cities, Harappa and Mohenjo-daro, had up to 50,000 people, when most large cities elsewhere had only 10,000. Oddly, there were no temples or palaces. Little is known about the Indus Valley's history.

Skara Brae homes had turf roofs

3100–2500 BCE

Homes in **Skara Brae**, Scotland, were made from stone layered with earth. Their furniture was also made of stone.

3000–1700 BCE

The **Longshan culture** flourished around the Yellow River in China, where the fertile soil made crops productive. It's famous for its highly polished black pottery. A surviving platform for observing the Sun shows us that the Longshan studied astronomy.

3000–1100 BCE

The Minoans on Crete were the first **European civilization**. They made maze-like palaces, fine jewelry and pottery, and vivid frescoes showing daily life.

2670 BCE

The **step pyramid of Djoser** was the first Egyptian pyramid. At 62 m (204 ft) tall, it was the highest structure of its time.

The Djoser pyramid was built by piling up massive stone blocks

2613–2181 BCE

In the "Old Kingdom" of Ancient Egypt, most kings demanded vast **pyramids** as memorial tombs. These took huge amounts of work and materials to build.

2550 BCE

The stones were put in place at **Stonehenge**, in southern England, although the site was probably in use from 3100 BCE. The entrance to the central circle lined up with sunrise at midsummer and sunset at midwinter.

Massive stones weighing up to 4,000 kg (9,000 lb) were hauled 300 km (185 miles) to make Stonehenge

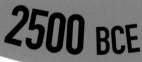

2500 BCE

c. 2500–350 BCE

The Kingdom of Kush in Nubia (now Sudan and Egypt) developed an advanced civilization in which **women played a more prominent role** than elsewhere in the ancient world.

The Great Sphinx is 73 m (240 ft) long and 20 m (66 ft) high

2558–2532 BCE

The mysterious **Great Sphinx of Giza**, located in Egypt, was probably carved during the reign of Khafre, but might be older. No one knows its purpose. It was the largest statue in the world.

2500 BCE

Ancient Egyptians began to **mummify their dead**. They removed the internal organs and used preservative chemicals, before wrapping the body in linen bandages.

A painted mask often covered the face of an Egyptian mummy

15

THE START OF HISTORY

History begins with the written record of events. Writing developed independently in several cultures around the world, and we know most about those cultures that left writing we can read. That doesn't mean that cultures without writing, or whose writing we can't yet decipher, knew less or were less sophisticated or advanced—we simply know less about them.

THE FERTILE CRESCENT

The "Fertile Crescent" is the area around the rivers Tigris, Euphrates, and Nile that was home to the Mesopotamian and Egyptian civilizations. The first writing developed here around 3400–3300 BCE. In Mesopotamia (in Iraq), people used a stick called a **stylus** to press wedge-shaped marks into soft clay **tablets**. The tablets were then baked to harden them. Many thousands of clay tablets have survived. This type of writing is called **cuneiform**. It used symbols to represent the sounds that make up words. The Sumerians used cuneiform for official documents and accounts, but also for poetry, medical texts, astronomical accounts, and records of events.

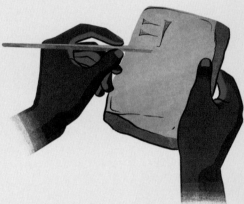

Soon after, around 3250–3200 BCE, Egyptian scribes began using a type of picture writing. Symbols began as recognizable images of objects, such as a foot, a bowl, or an eagle. They were called **hieroglyphs** when carved in stone, and **hieratic** when written with reed pens or brushes on papyrus. Over time, the symbols became more stylized. Some symbols represented sounds, and some showed which of several meanings a word had. These sound-characters were the ancestors of later European alphabets.

AROUND THE WORLD

Mesopotamia and Egypt were close together, and writing in one place perhaps influenced its development nearby. People in **China** developed writing independently with no clear path to join them to the Fertile Crescent. The people of **Mesoamerica** made their own writing systems around 900–600 BCE with no link to Europe, Asia, or Africa. The Chinese character system was pictographic, again starting with pictures that later became less recognizable. The earliest Chinese characters are inscribed on "oracle bones"—shards of bone or tortoise shell used to try to predict what the future might bring. China had a fully functional writing system by 1300 BCE.

The early character for mountains (top) looks like a mountain range, but the modern character (bottom) is more stylized

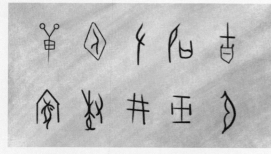

Chinese characters from oracle bones, around 1500 BCE

GLYPHS AND STRINGS

In Mesoamerica (from Mexico to Costa Rica), the Mayans used **glyphs** painted onto codices (books) made of deer skin or tree bark, or carved into stone. Few of these books survive, as many were destroyed by European invaders in the 1500s. One unique way of recording numbers, and possibly also words, was the **quipu** made of knotted strings hanging from a backbone string. The quipu code has not yet been interpreted.

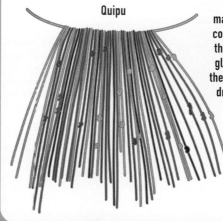

Quipu

Glyphs (above) were made by putting different components together. The three components of this glyph (top) are shown by the blue, green, and yellow drawings underneath it.

MYSTERIES REMAIN

The **Indus Valley** civilization left many stone seals, but these have not been decoded. There are only 400 known characters, which is too few for a system that uses a different symbol for each word. Wooden tablets from **Rapa Nui** (Easter Island), called "rongorongo" use 120 glyphs to produce texts up to 2,320 characters long, but their meaning has been lost. Writing might have emerged independently here, too.

A stone seal from the Indus Valley, around 2000 BCE

2499–1500 BCE

Some cities grew, taking over surrounding land and settlements, and becoming kingdoms and empires. But large communities were vulnerable to disasters such as floods, failing crops, disease, and attack from others. Some cities and kingdoms fell. Those that survived produced the first literature and astronomy, and some important inventions that made these civilizations even more successful.

2000 BCE

The Indus Valley civilization **tamed elephants**. They used them for forestry work, in wars, and in ceremonies.

2000 BCE

The last **woolly mammoths died** on Wrangel Island, which is located in the Arctic Ocean. The iconic ice age mammals that lived in the unique environment on the island had survived thousands of years longer than those on the mainland, but eventually they too died out, due to a combination of different factors.

2334–2279 BCE

Sargon of Akkad created the first empire in **Mesopotamia**, bringing together several kingdoms. Efficient and widespread administration helped it succeed.

c. 2030 BCE

The earliest **code of laws**, the Code of Ur-Nammu, was produced in Sumer. Some crimes were punishable by death, but most brought only a fine.

2499 BCE

2285–2250 BCE

The first known named **author**, the Mesopotamian poet Enheduanna, was probably the daughter of Sargon of Akkad.

2150–1400 BCE

Gilgamesh was written—the oldest epic in world literature. It tells of Gilgamesh's journey to seek eternal life after the death of his friend.

2180 BCE

The **Old Kingdom in Egypt collapsed**. Civil war, drought, and famine ravaged the land until the Middle Kingdom was founded in 2040 BCE.

1900–1500 BCE

The **Indus Valley civilization declined**, perhaps because of climate change, the drying of the Sarasvati River, and falling trade with Egypt.

1800 BCE

The Mesopotamian army used **war chariots**, allowing soldiers to shoot arrows at enemies while moving. Horse-drawn chariots were used from around 2000 BCE in the Steppe, before people began to ride on horseback.

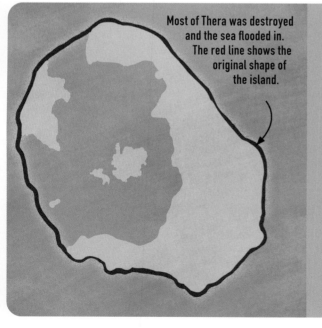

The Olmec made giant stone heads

c. 1750–1500 BCE

Assyrian astronomers in northern Mesopotamia identified the **five planets** readily visible to the naked eye: Mercury, Venus, Mars, Jupiter, and Saturn. Some of the names they gave to constellations of stars are still used today.

1500–200 BCE

The **Olmec civilization**, in the Gulf of Mexico, built great cities of stone and brick. They were the first culture in South America.

1500 BCE

1795–1750 BCE

The Babylonian **Code of Hammurabi** set out punishments for a wide range of crimes, demanding like-for-like physical penalties such as "an eye for an eye."

1700–1100 BCE

Indigenous Americans made **Poverty Point**, a huge system of earthworks, with a large mound and concentric semicircles.

c. 1600 BCE

The first historical Chinese dynasty, the **Shang**, began.

Most of Thera was destroyed and the sea flooded in. The red line shows the original shape of the island.

c. 1650–1550 BCE

A **volcano** on the Greek island of **Thera** (Santorini) erupted catastrophically, blowing the island apart. Earthquakes, giant waves, and a thick blanket of ash destroyed settlements in nearby lands. It was the most powerful eruption of the last 10,000 years.

1500 BCE

People in South America first domesticated and grew **cocoa beans**.

1500 BCE

The first writings in Sanskrit, the Vedas, laid down the basics of the **Hindu religion**. The Indian caste system began at this time, dividing people into different social levels depending on the type of work did, and dictating what they were allowed to do.

CHINESE DYNASTIES

A dynasty is a ruling family that passes down leadership from one generation to the next. Dynasties have been common around the world, from the Egyptian pharaohs to European royal families, but perhaps the most famous are those from China. The history of China is traditionally divided into dynasties, with the start of a new dynasty beginning a new chapter in the history of the land.

GETTING STARTED

The first Chinese dynasty, the **Xia**, is considered mythical by many historians. It supposedly started with Yu the Great around 2100 BCE and lasted until around 1600 BCE, when the first dynasty that has been historically verified began. Yu is said to have made China stable and wealthy by controlling flood waters with irrigation channels.

The first historical dynasty, the **Shang**, started after the Shang leader Tang overthrew the tyrant Jie. The Shang created a stable government and encouraged many advances, including a standardized writing system, industrial casting of bronze, a 365-day calendar, and religious rituals. The Shang dynasty ended in 1046 BCE when the emperor **Zhou**, who had become a lazy, self-indulgent tyrant, was overthrown by King Wu of the province Zhou.

The legendary Yu the Great

CHANGING HANDS

Chinese rulers claimed to rule by virtue of the **Mandate of Heaven**, beginning with the Zhou dynasty. Supposedly, the heavens chose a just ruler and supported him, so to overthrow him would mean defying the heavens. But if the heavens were displeased with a ruler, terrible things could happen, such as earthquakes, famines, and rebellions. These were taken as signs that the emperor had lost the mandate of heaven and a new ruler should be chosen, starting another dynasty. The system made **astrology** very important to the Chinese, as events in the heavens were thought to have an impact on events on Earth.

An unexpected event, such as a comet, could be taken as a bad omen—a sign the heavens were displeased with an emperor

WRITING IT DOWN

Oracle bone script

We know about the Shang dynasty because the first Chinese writing comes from this time, inscribed on **oracle bones**. Priests scratched questions into the bones, then heated them to make them crack. From the pattern of cracks, they tried to work out the gods' answers to the questions. Objects and writings from a historic time are valuable to historians as "primary sources"—direct evidence of what happened.

BETWEEN DYNASTIES

Early dynastic rule wasn't stable. China covers a large area, and it was impossible for a leader to keep control of it all the time. In the **Spring and Autumn Period** of 770–475 BCE and the following **Warring States Period**, many local leaders began fighting between themselves. At times, there were over 1,000 small states; by the end of the Warring States Period, warlords had gathered these together into seven major states at war with each other.

CHINA UNITED

The extent of the Chinese state under the Xia, Zhou, and Qin dynasties

Xia dynasty

The seven states were eventually brought under the control of a single ruler—Shi Huangdi, who became the first **Qin** emperor in 221 BCE. In 230 BCE, the Han state surrendered to Qin, afraid of attack. The next state, Wei, surrendered after Shi diverted a river to flood the main city, causing devastation. Shi quickly took over the remaining states. He united China and held it together by a mix of military force, moving all power to the central administration, and removing borders between states. The name "China" comes from "Qin" (pronounced "chin").

Although Shi's rule was short (he died in 210 BCE), the united imperial China he built remained until the end of the last dynasty, the Qing, in 1912.

Zhou dynasty

Qin dynasty

■ Extent under the named dynasty

Extent of modern China

FORMS OF GOVERNMENT

We know little about how the earliest social groups were organized, but from the start of history, it seems that most cultures had a chieftain or king in charge. We would now call this system a monarchy. As civilizations grew larger and more complex, they needed more complicated forms of civic organization and more bureaucracy (rules, staff, and systems) to keep them running.

HUNTING, GATHERING, AND MOVING

Before the start of farming, people lived in small groups of to up to 100 individuals. They moved around the land, hunting animals and collecting roots, fruit, nuts, and seeds to eat. Cooperation was important, but little formal organization was needed. **Hunter-gatherer communities** continued in some places until around 1500 CE, but few survive now. One existing group is the Hadza in Tanzania. The social structure of the Hadza people includes different "bands" that have no hierarchy (tiers of authority or wealth). Instead, decisions are reached communally by discussion. Earlier hunter-gatherers perhaps lived in a similar way.

SETTLED AND STRUCTURED

Larger, settled groups needed much more organization than a hunter-gatherer tribe. When each person was no longer searching for their own food and making their own weapons and tools, society needed a structure that would **share out work and property**.

A VOICE OF AUTHORITY

Larger communities often developed a **hierarchy**, with one person or group having more wealth and power than others. At first, it might have been the person who was physically stronger or could gather more supporters who took charge. This **chieftain** or **monarch** then had the authority to organize the society in a way that kept them in power. They were often in danger of being overthrown, either by someone within the group, or by outsiders. The role of chief or monarch was often hereditary, and passed down a family line. The remains of many early settlements include palaces that apparently belonged to a leader. Even when there are no written records to tell us how a community was run, grand buildings and fine objects suggest someone was monarch.

Statue of an early South American chieftain, 300–600 CE

KINGS, GODS, AND EMPERORS

In some places, kings claimed the authority of a **god** to support their rule. In ancient Egypt, part of the pharaoh's role was to attend religious ceremonies, keeping peace with the gods. As a civic leader, the pharaoh made laws, decided when the country should go to war, and collected taxes to pay for public goods.

Some rulers even claimed to be directly descended from gods. This made it difficult for rivals to challenge their position. If the emperor had divine approval or was a god, rebelling against him became spiritually, as well as physically, dangerous. The emperors of Japan claimed descent from the sun god.

BY THE PEOPLE, FOR THE PEOPLE

A new approach to government began in ancient Athens at the end of the 6th century BCE. It was the start of **democracy**—a form of government in which the people either make political decisions themselves, as a group, or they elect representatives to make decisions for them. This saw a move away from rule by a very small group (such as a royal family or the very wealthy) to rule by public consent. Athenian democracy was not like modern democracy, as only free men (not slaves or women) were allowed to vote.

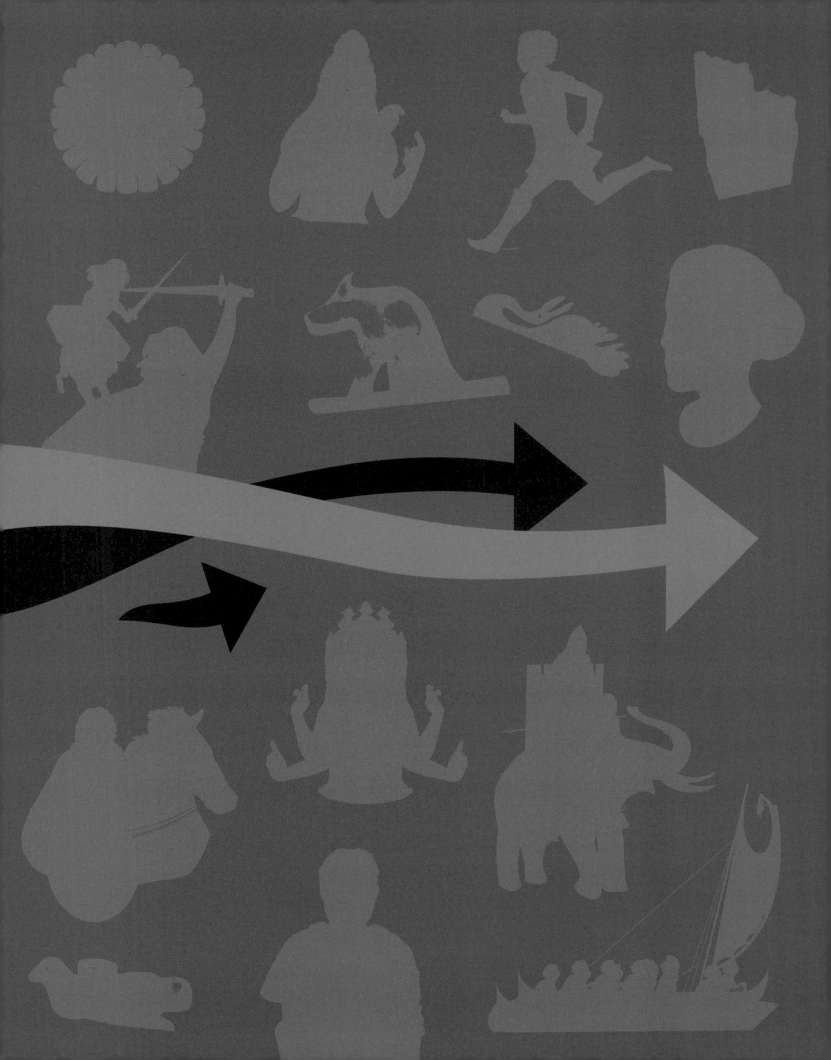

CHAPTER 2

THE ANCIENT WORLD

The 1,000 years around the start of the Common Era (CE) saw huge changes around the world. It was a time of mighty empires rising and falling. It also saw the great religions of the world coming into place—and sometimes pitting themselves against each other.

We have detailed histories of the events, wars, and campaigns of the Mediterranean and Middle Eastern powers, of China, and North Africa. We know the names of important figures in these regions, and sometimes we have several accounts of events left by different groups. This is especially useful to historians, as different accounts of events rarely agree fully. Historians look for evidence of what happened and why—yet the accounts are often biased toward showing an individual's or group's own actions in a good light. Having more than one account, particularly from opposing sides of battles and disputes, helps historians to build a fuller picture.

Some parts of the world, though, still left few or no written records, and we know less of what happened there. For instance, we don't know about the events that shaped some of the cultures of North and South America, Australasia, Russia, the Arctic, and much of Africa.

ALEXANDER THE GREAT

One of the most important figures of the late centuries BCE was Alexander the Great. A military leader from Macedonia, Greece, he built a vast empire, and spread Greek culture as far as India.

FATHER OF A CONQUEROR

Philip II of Macedon, Alexander's father, became king of Macedonia in 359 BCE. He **reformed the army** to march in closely packed rectangular blocks (phalanxes) of foot soldiers armed with spears and protected with shields. This strategy made them hard to defeat, and he conquered most of Greece. He planned to invade the Persian Empire but was murdered in 336 BCE.

As a young man, Philip II of Macedon lost his right eye in battle

CONQUERING HERO

The dark red area shows the extent of Alexander's empire

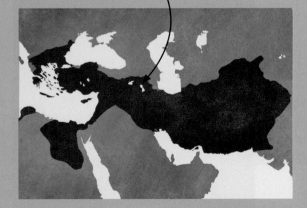

Alexander (356–323 BCE) was only 20 years old when he took over his father's kingdom in 336 BCE. Following his father's plan to conquer the Persian Empire, he led his army through Egypt, Syria, and Iraq, without ever suffering defeat. At the age of just 25, after a glorious victory at the Battle of Gaugamela (336 BCE), he was king of Greece, ruler of Asia Minor, pharaoh of Egypt, and king of Persia. He marched farther east, building an empire that stretched from the River Danube in Europe to the River Ganges in India. His military expeditions were bold, and he won against almost impossible odds. Finally, in India, his troops would go no farther, wanting to return home. Alexander died of fever in Babylon at the age of 33. By then, he had built the **greatest empire the world had ever seen**.

In India, Alexander's army encountered war elephants

Alexander named a city after his beloved warhorse, Bucephalus

NEW WORLDS

Alexander was more than just a brilliant soldier. The Greek philosopher Aristotle had been his personal tutor, and Alexander grew into a **cultured and curious man**. He took scientists to the lands he conquered to investigate the new plants, animals, and geology. He brought cultures together, spreading Greek learning and practices, but also adapting to and respecting local practices. In Egypt, he restored Egyptian temples and made offerings to the gods at Memphis; in Persia, he adopted elements of court dress and customs. But he was principally a conqueror. His army slaughtered defeated soldiers and sold women and children as slaves. He allowed the great Persian city Persepolis to burn, and destroyed and looted many other great cities.

CULTURE WARS

War often causes only destruction, but Alexander built many cities in the lands he took. One of the first and greatest was **Alexandria** in Egypt. It became the capital of Egypt. By spreading Greek culture and language widely, Alexander began the age of Hellenistic (Greek) Egypt. For 300 years, areas of the Middle East used the Greek language and continued to develop Greek culture, now combined with that of Egypt, Persia, and Mesopotamia. This rich cross-fertilization laid the foundations for the intellectual development of Europe, North Africa and the Near East over the next 2,000 years. When Alexander died in 323 BCE, the empire soon broke up, with fighting over it continuing for 40 years.

The amphitheater at Ai-Khanoum, on the borders of Russia and Afghanistan, is an example of Greek architecture far from Greece

RISE OF THE ROMAN EMPIRE

Rome began as a single city near the west coast of Italy, yet by the end of the 1st century CE it ruled 30 percent of the world's population—4–5 million people.

ROMAN REPUBLIC

In 509 BCE, the last king of Rome, Tarquinius, was overthrown at the end of a long process of change. The city-state was then ruled by the "patricians," the men of notable, wealthy families. This annoyed the other citizens, who objected. After 494 BCE, power was shared among more (male) citizens. Over time, a complicated structure developed of assemblies and elected officials who governed Rome and decided its laws and policies. It had become a **Republic**.

The purple zone is the largest area ruled by the Roman Empire

THE RISE OF ROME

Originally, Italy was a collection of city-states that fought over land and borders. Rome forced men into military service, and by 275 BCE the army had taken over most of Italy and developed methods of war that made it unbeatable. Rome grew to be the main power in the Mediterranean after the defeat of **Carthage** in the Punic Wars (264–146 BCE) and of **Greece** in the Macedonian Wars (214–148 BCE).

A MILITARY POWER

The **Roman army** was divided into troops trained and organized for different types of fighting, with carefully thought-out tactics and a tiered structure of leadership. There were three levels of foot soldiers (legionaries) and then cavalry (horse-riding soldiers). Soldiers were sent into battle in increasing order of expertise and weaponry, saving the best warriors for last. This meant the enemy were hit by increasingly experienced fresh troops during a battle.

From 107 BCE, the commander **Gaius Marius** made huge changes to the army. For the first time, soldiers didn't have to own property or buy their own weapons and armor, but were trained and equipped with a spear and sword by the state. It became a regular standing army, growing quickly as men flocked to join. The soldiers were grouped into four legions of 6,000 men each. Each carried his own equipment, removing the need for a baggage train. Gaius Marius recruited soldiers from conquered lands, who often had special skills suited to fighting in their own regions.

In the "tortoise" formation, groups of foot soldiers went into battle fully protected in front and above by large shields

FROM REPUBLIC TO EMPIRE

The reform of the army had some unplanned results. Soldiers relied on their generals for payment, and became more loyal to them than to the state. Power struggles between generals became common. Corruption and threats led to three men forming a "triumvirate" to take control of Rome: **Julius Caesar**, **Pompey**, and **Crassus**. But it didn't last. Crassus was killed in battle, and Pompey died when he went to war with Julius Caesar. The survivor, Caesar, was declared dictator (sole ruler). When he was murdered, the Republic collapsed and gave way to the **Roman Empire**. The first emperor, in 27 BCE, was Caesar's stepson, **Augustus**.

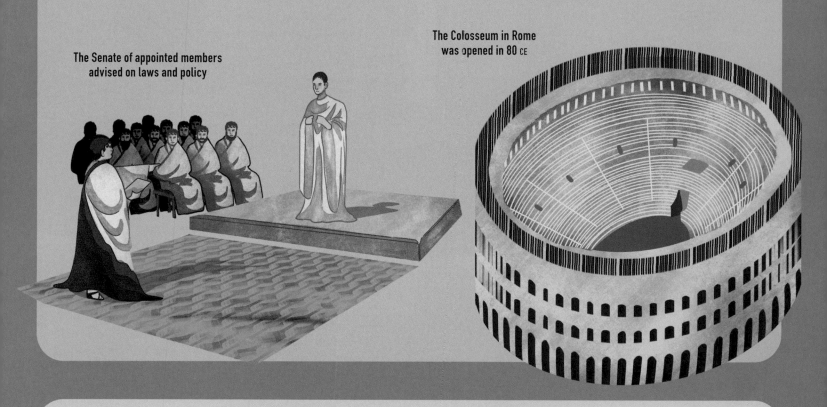

The Senate of appointed members advised on laws and policy

The Colosseum in Rome was opened in 80 CE

ROMAN EUROPE

The Roman Empire prospered for a long time, reaching its height in 117 CE as the **largest empire of the western world**. The Romans built good-quality roads throughout their conquered lands, aqueducts to carry water channels, and buildings that in some cases have lasted until today. They spread the Latin language and Roman civilization throughout their empire, from northern England to Turkey and North Africa.

CHAPTER 3

THE MIDDLE AGES

The period between the death of Muhammad and 1400 saw the "Old World" of Europe, Asia, and Africa becoming much more connected, but there were still no links between the Old World and the Americas or Australasia. This period, commonly called the Middle Ages, saw huge changes in much of the world. Struggles between Islam and Christianity played out in the Middle East. In the Far East, China, Japan, and Korea forged identities that have shaped them as modern nations. It was a time of empire-building on a grand scale, and often bitter warfare.

The Mongol Empire stretched from China to the middle of Europe at its height, and much of West Africa fell under the control of the Mali Empire. Europe became Christian, and launched a terrible assault on the Muslim Arabs—a century of "Crusades" to claim the holy area of Jerusalem and Israel as their own. But the most turmoil came at the end of the period, with the Black Death, a deadly pandemic that swept through Europe and parts of Asia, killing millions.

LASTING RELIGIONS

Early religions were often polytheistic (meaning they have many gods), and some focused on spirits in streams, trees, and other natural features. Of the religions that have survived, most are monotheistic (they have one god), and many became established in 350 BCE to 650 CE.

ZOROASTRIANISM

Zoroastrianism began between 1500 BCE and 1000 BCE in Iran, founded by the Persian prophet **Zoroaster** who was enlightened by a vision. Its single god, **Ahura Mazda**, is worshipped through good thoughts, good words, and good deeds. Zoroastrianism grew from a polytheistic religion in which Ahura Mazda was the chief god. Zoroaster's teachings were passed down by word of mouth until the 6th century BCE, when they were written down. Zoroastrianism had a heaven and hell, a judgment day at the end of time, and other aspects adopted by later religions, including Christianity and Islam.

The Zoroastrian god
Ahura Mazda

Yahweh spoke to Moses from a burning bush, commanding him to lead the Israelites out of Egypt

JUDAISM

Early Judaism (the religion of the Jews) separated from older Israelite religions sometime in the 6th century BCE, leaving **Yahweh** as the only god by the 3rd century BCE. The Hebrew Bible tells the history of the Israelites, starting with the creation of the world, and sets down the laws by which Jews must live. The most important prophets in Judaism are **Abraham** and **Moses**. Yahweh gave Moses the most important laws, the Ten Commandments, written on stone tablets.

CHRISTIANITY

Christianity started after the death of **Jesus Christ** around 30 CE. The Christian **Bible** consists of the Old and New Testaments, the second of which records the life of Jesus Christ. The Old Testament is shared with Judaism. Christians consider Christ to be the **Messiah**, sent to free humankind and cleanse them of sin, fulfilling a prophesy in the Old Testament. Jews consider Christ to be another prophet, and believe that the Messiah has not yet come.

A Byzantine mosaic of Christ

ISLAM

Islam shares Old Testament stories with Judaism and Christianity, but sees **Muhammad** as the last prophet sent by God (**Allah**). **Muslims** (followers of Islam) believe that Allah dictated the holy **Quran** to Muhammad in the 7th century CE. Other important prophets were Abraham, Moses, and Jesus. Muslims are taught to pray daily, give to charity, fast during the month of Ramadan, and go on a pilgrimage to Mecca at least once.

A pilgrimage to the Kaaba, or House of God, in Mecca, is called "hajj." The Kaaba is a cube-shaped building in the middle of the Masjid al-Haram mosque.

BUDDHISM

Buddhism began in India in the 5th century BCE with the teachings of the **Buddha**, a prince who left his life of luxury and went out into the world to seek truth. Prompted by seeing the sufferings of ordinary people, the prince meditated and sought nlightenment, which came to him as he sat under a tree. He spent the rest of his life teaching people to live a virtuous life. Buddhists try to live according to the teachings of Buddha.

HINDUISM

Hinduism is a diverse and varied religion that began around 2000 BCE in the Indus Valley. The main god is **Brahman**, who Hindus believe is present everywhere and takes many forms. His most important forms are as creator (**Brahma**), preserver of the world (**Vishnu**), and destroyer (**Shiva**). Hindus believe in a cycle of life, death, and rebirth, and that the world is periodically destroyed and renewed. Hinduism has several sacred texts, including stories of the gods and hymns of praise.

MONGOL EMPIRE

The Mongols were tribes from the Central Asian Steppe, perhaps originating in Kazakhstan. Originally nomads, they lived on horseback and were used to the harshest weather and living conditions. This gave them a great advantage when they set out to conquer lands from China to Europe. Over the 13th century, the Mongols built the largest empire the world had ever seen.

FIRST STEPPES

Temujin (c. 1162–1227) rose from a harsh childhood to become military leader of the Kerait tribe. He drew in or conquered other tribes until a meeting of tribal leaders recognized him as **Genghis Khan**, "universal leader," in 1206. Combining the forces of all the tribes, he had a formidable army of horsemen. He adopted the script of the Uighur Turks to make a written form of Mongolian, which previously had no writing. Then he set about building an empire. His son and successor, Ogedei Khan, continued the expansion of the Mongol Empire eastward, and conquered the Kingdom of Goryeo (Korea) in 1231.

HEADING WEST

From 1218, Genghis Khan also sent his warriors westward, first sweeping through Persia, then northern Afghanistan (1221), then Russia near the Caspian Sea (1223). By the time Genghis Khan died of illness in 1227, he was known by the Muslims in conquered regions as **the accursed one**. His army was brutal and pitiless. Wherever they went, they destroyed cities and slaughtered the inhabitants, burning the buildings and wrecking irrigation systems to make farming impossible. The reputation of the Mongols for brutality meant that cities would often surrender without a fight, afraid of what would befall them otherwise.

A MIGHTY EMPIRE

Genghis Khan had wanted his four sons to rule after him, but one had already died. Of the remaining three, **Ogedei** became the great Khan and supreme ruler. He continued to expand the empire, but also strengthened the land he had. He introduced a proper system of taxes, appointed regional governors, and built a capital at Karakorum. In the east, he defeated the Jin dynasty in China and raided Korea repeatedly. In the west, the Mongols reached eastern Europe, sacking and looting Kyiv in Ukraine (1240), Kraków in Poland (1241), and Buda and Pest in Hungary (1241). Only Ogedei's death stopped them going farther west.

The Mongols were expert archers

Modern China

Extent ruled by the Yuan dynasty

ANOTHER GREAT KHAN

When Genghis Khan's grandson, **Kublai**, came to power in 1260, expansion continued. Although the empire was technically still split into four, Kublai had the larger part. His heart was set on greater things, though. He attacked China, this time using siege warfare, and defeated one city after another, including the capital in 1276. With the fall of the Song dynasty, Kublai was declared emperor of China, starting the **Yuan dynasty** of occupation. Attacks on Japan were not as successful. The Japanese survived two assaults, in 1274 and 1281, when Japanese resistance and terrible storms destroyed Mongolian ships. Attacks on Vietnam, Java, and Burma were only partly successful.

DEATH OF AN EMPIRE

The four regions of the original empire slowly decayed. In eastern Europe and Russia, the **Golden Horde** (originally the northwest part of the Mongol empire) lasted longest, until 1502, but internal and border disputes ate away at all the khanates. In China, civil wars, famine, rebellion, and economic problems eventually led to the fall of the Yuan dynasty, to be replaced by the **Ming dynasty** in 1368.

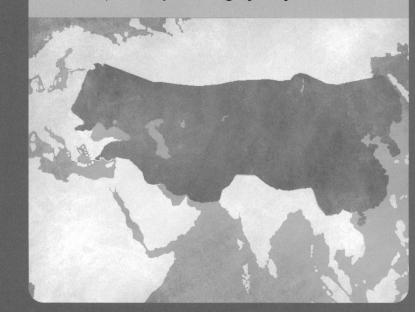

BLACK DEATH

The Black Death was a pandemic of bubonic plague and its variants that spread through Asia, North Africa, and Europe in the middle of the 14th century. Around two thirds of people who caught the disease died—up to half the population in affected areas, or at least 50 million people worldwide. The effects on individuals and societies were devastating, and the population of Europe took 200 years to grow back to pre-plague levels. Outbreaks of plague continued for hundreds of years.

The plague was both painful and terrifying for sufferers

RATS, FLEAS, AND BOILS

Bubonic plague is a disease caused by **bacteria**. It's often spread by fleas that usually live on rats and other rodents. If a flea carrying plague bacteria bites someone, the person can catch plague. The disease can also spread directly between people, producing slightly different forms of the illness. Sufferers during the Black Death had fever and joint pain, followed by a rash, and then extremely painful boils that sometimes turned hard and black, giving the pandemic its name.

PLAGUE FROM THE EAST

The plague probably began in Central Asia, Mongolia, China, or India, and was carried east and west by Mongol warriors and traders. It entered Europe in 1347 through the Mediterranean sea ports and Crimea. It spread west and north over the next five years, leaving a **trail of devastation**. The effects were uneven, with some places barely affected, but some towns and villages entirely destroyed.

☐ 1347	☐ 1350	
☐ 1348	☐ 1351	
☐ 1349	☐ Unaffected	

Plague spread from the east in 1346, taking hold over most of Europe in 1348–1350

The "Dance of Death" was a common scene in art

SOCIAL CHAOS

The effects of the pandemic were devastating. With so many dying, there were **not enough people** to dig graves for all the dead, who were piled into large pits. There were too few people to work the farms, so crops rotted or were never planted, and farm animals died or wandered away. In the years after the plague, the surviving workers could demand more money and better conditions. The feudal system relying on serfs who were tied to working the land of their overlords collapsed in many places. Serfs were replaced by peasants who could move between employers. Rebellions, food shortages, and civil unrest continued for decades after the worst of the plague was over.

TERRIFYING MYSTERY

At the time, people didn't know about bacteria or understand **how diseases spread**. Many feared it was spread by "bad air," and others thought that the plague was a punishment sent by God. Some people prayed for relief, promised to build churches, or whipped themselves as a form of self-punishment to atone for past sins. The art and literature of the time shows people being aware that life was fragile and death ever-present.

People were so afraid of plague that they would flee their towns and villages to avoid it, but many carried it with them to the places they ran away to. By moving around, they **spread the plague** farther and faster. There were no effective treatments for plague at the time, though now it can be treated with antibiotics.

Some people were buried in coffins in a ceremonial way, but many were piled into mass graves

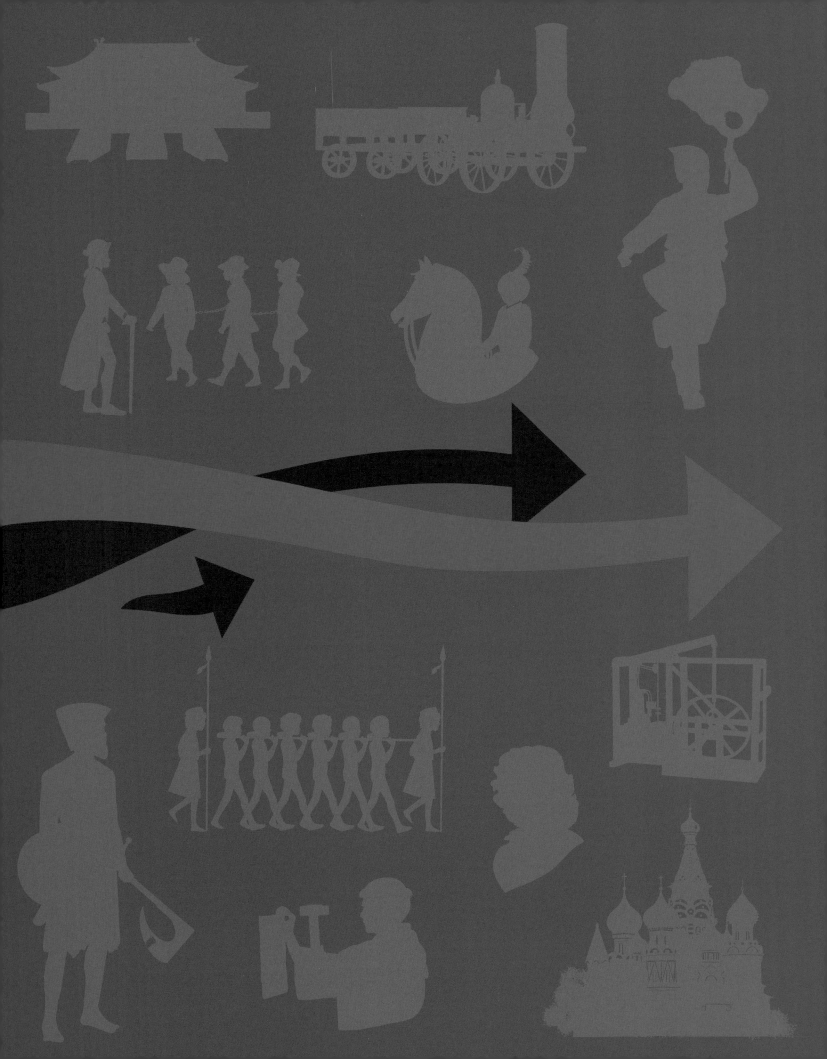

CHAPTER 4

CONNECTING THE WORLD

The middle of the 15th century saw the start of the "Age of Discovery," when European adventurers set off across the oceans and found lands they previously knew nothing about. Using overland routes for trade between Europe and Asia was difficult, so sailors went in search of sea routes to India, China, and beyond. On the way, they found the Americas. Later explorers came across Australia.

The Europeans didn't recognize the rights of the people already living in these lands. They saw these places as new and undiscovered areas they could plunder and colonize. Invaders stole the land, killed and enslaved the inhabitants, plundered civilizations, and destroyed their cultures. At the same time, they carried animals, plants, and diseases between the "Old World" of Europe, Africa, and Asia and the "New World" of North and South America and the Caribbean islands. The invaders' unfamiliar diseases, including flu, measles, and smallpox, killed millions of people who had no resistance to them.

CLOSED WORLDS

While Europeans were exploring and conquering the world, the Far East became closed and solitary. Trade with the rest of the world was cut, and over a period of several centuries China, Japan, and Korea swayed between complete isolation, with closed borders, and just limited access to foreign influences.

PIRATES AHOY!

Korea and Japan were terrorized by **wokou pirates** based around Japan from the 13th century. They attacked ships at sea and coastal settlements in Japan, Korea, and later China. Raids could involve 400 ships, and 3,000 attackers taking goods and seizing people who were sold into slavery. To avoid raiders, farming communities moved farther inland, losing good farmland. Piracy was a risky business, though—if caught, the punishment was death.

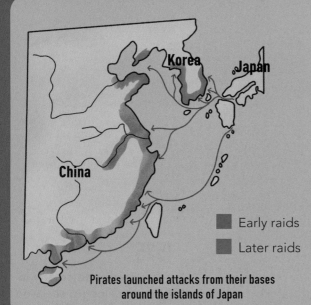

Pirates launched attacks from their bases around the islands of Japan

- Early raids
- Later raids

CLOSING THE DOOR

When building forts along the coast and tackling pirate ships at sea didn't work, the Chinese **banned sea trade** in 1371, and destroyed ships and dockyards starting in 1384. Any remaining ship was considered a pirate ship and could be attacked. But real traders became so desperate that piracy increased. Piracy in China only reduced after the ban on trade was lifted in 1567. Similar bans were reintroduced in the 1600s, and were more strictly enforced. Japan and Korea also took the same measure at different times, cutting off or restricting trade with the outside world. From 1633 to 1853, Japan's policy of "sakoku" ("chained country") largely restricted trade to China and Korea.

PORTUGAL IN THE EAST

The **Portuguese** were the first Europeans to enter China by sea, arriving in Guangzhou in 1517. The Portuguese were allowed to build a trading post at Macau, land that remained Portuguese from 1557 until 1999. While China was closed to trade, Macau was the only port allowing trade with Japan. Portugal dominated trade between India, Indonesia, China, and Japan.

In 1543, three Portuguese traders whose ship had been blown off course became the first Europeans in Japan, and more followed. This early Portuguese influence introduced firearms (the musket) to Japan, and allowed the entry of Jesuits (Catholic priests) who converted some Japanese people to Christianity, beginning in 1549. Portuguese traders and Jesuits were allowed to settle and trade. But with the "chained country" policy beginning in 1633, openness ended. All foreign trade went through an artificial island, **Dejima**, built in Nagasaki. No foreign traders were allowed into mainland Japan, and Christianity was banned. The Portuguese were thrown out of Dejima in 1639, and after that only Dutch traders were allowed until 1854.

The island of Dejima was just 120 m (395 ft long)

SCIENCE AND RELIGION

One of the first westerners known to learn Chinese was the Italian Jesuit **Matteo Ricci**. He was also the first to write a Chinese dictionary for western use, and the first westerner allowed into the Forbidden City in Beijing. He translated some Chinese classic texts into Latin, making a two-way intellectual exchange between Europe and China. Ricci and other Jesuits introduced both Christianity and the learning of western scientists into China. Western astronomy, in particular, was very different from Chinese astronomy, which was focused on making accurate calendars and trying to match events in the heavens to events on Earth.

SELLING HUMANS: SLAVERY

People have enslaved others for thousands of years. The Sumerians, Greeks, ancient Chinese, and many other early civilizations relied heavily on slavery for building, farming, and domestic work. Enslaved people often endured terrible conditions, especially in the 18th and 19th centuries.

Enslaved people were often traded at markets, and were considered the property of the person who bought them

BEING ENSLAVED

There were several ways people could become enslaved. Some may have been born into slavery, the children of an enslaved mother. Others may have been part of a group that was defeated by a conquering army. Sometimes, people who lived near a coast—anywhere from southern Ireland to China and Japan—were at risk. Pirates raided inland and snatched people who were then sold as slaves.

In the Middle Ages, the church forbade the sale of Christian slaves and so the slave trade clustered around markets in the middle east. The most extreme recent exploitation of enslaved people was the capture and sale of **Black Africans** to work in the **New World**.

OUT OF AFRICA

European invaders took land in South and North America and in the Caribbean, and began to grow crops. But a shortage of workers willing or able to do the hard work of farming in a hot environment soon led landowners into a terrible trade. From the 1570s, when Portugal opened a trading post for enslaved African people in Angola, **European colonists shipped enslaved African people across the Atlantic**. Although Arab slave traders mounted their own expeditions into Africa to capture people, European traders rarely went far inland. Instead, they bought enslaved people from African chieftains and traders. Several African kingdoms relied on the sale of their own captured enemies and rivals as a source of income.

THE TRANSATLANTIC SLAVE TRADE

Enslaved people were chained and marched to ports, where they were packed into ships and taken over the ocean. They endured horrific conditions, treated as cargo rather than human beings. Often, between 10 and 20 percent died on the sea crossing. Once in the Americas, these people were sold to work on **plantations** growing crops such as sugar, coffee, tobacco, and cotton, or to work as **domestic servants**.

The trade made a great deal of money for the owners of ships that followed a triangular route. The ships first carried goods such as iron, cloth, and guns from Europe to Africa, where they were sold, and the hold was packed with captured people. The enslaved people were taken to the New World for sale, and the ships were restocked with items such as sugar, tobacco, and cotton to return to Europe. Few enslaved people were taken from Africa to Europe; those who did end up in Europe usually served as domestic servants and were often treated as an exotic oddity.

People were packed into slave ships as though they were objects

LIFE AS AN ENSLAVED PERSON

Enslaved people were considered to be **property**. They could be physically abused, shackled and chained, sold on to other owners, refused permission to marry, have their children taken away, and be treated in any other way the enslaver chose. Enslaved Africans had no rights. Many worked on plantations growing crops such as sugar and (later) cotton. The work was hard, and the enslaved people were watched over and often whipped or beaten by overseers to make sure they carried on working.

INDUSTRIAL REVOLUTION

While revolutions in France, Haiti, America, and South America changed the lives of people in those places, the Industrial Revolution eventually changed the whole world. Beginning in Britain around 1750, it produced the modern world of mechanized and industrialized production of goods on a large scale.

STARTING WITH FUEL

At first, water power was used to drive machinery, and the main fuel used was **wood**. But as more forests were cut down, wood became expensive. **Coal** became a more important fuel. The Industrial Revolution was possible in Britain because it had large natural deposits of coal.

In 1712, Thomas Newcomen invented a coal-powered **steam engine**. This could pump water from coal mines, making mining much more efficient. Steam engines were used to mine coal, which was used to power more steam engines! But steam engines could also be used to power other types of machinery. When James Watt improved the steam engine in the 1760s, its use in manufacturing really took off, starting with fabric-making.

James Watt's steam engine

FROM MINE TO FACTORY

Steam engines changed **transport** as well as the manufacturing industry. The first trains, in Wales in 1804, were used to move iron and coal from mines, but soon began moving other goods and people around. Steam engines were also used for boats and ships—and eventually a similar principle was used to make cars.

The DeWitt Clinton locomotive first ran in America in 1831

FROM FARM TO FACTORY

Children were often employed to drag trucks of coal in the mines, as they could fit through low, narrow tunnels deep underground

Before the Industrial Revolution, around 80 percent of the world's population worked farming food; today, around 1 or 2 percent of people in industrialized nations work in farming. Improvements in technology and better farming practices meant that more food could be produced more easily, with fewer workers. Many people who had worked in farming were forced to look for other work. Some went to work in the expanding coal mines; others moved into the cities, where the **factories** needed workers. But the new work was often performed in terrible conditions.

MINING ORES

The demand for coal meant more people had to work in the mines. But mining was not only for coal. The demand for **iron** to make machinery and other metals and chemicals used in industrial processes meant there was more mining of many types. The metal needed was then extracted from the ore and cast into metal objects in **foundries**. Here, people worked in intense heat with very dangerous molten metal.

FABRIC FIRST

One of the most important products of the Industrial Revolution was **cloth**. Spinning yarn and weaving were once time-consuming processes, but mechanization made them quick. Huge factory looms produced wool and cotton fabric quickly. **Cotton** was in particular demand. It had been imported from India, where low wages made producing cotton fabric cheap. But new factories made cheap manufacture possible in Britain. Cotton was grown in America by enslaved people, and was shipped to Britain for automated weaving. Working in the factories among huge, fast-moving machinery was dangerous and unpleasant.

UNHEALTHY LIVES

People worked long hours in harsh and dangerous conditions, and lived crowded together in sprawling **slums** of very poor-quality homes with little fresh air or space. The air in and around cities was polluted with smoke and fumes from the factories, the rivers were polluted with industrial waste, and many people suffered from bad health as a result. Wages were low, and people, including children, had to work many hours a day. Most children started work by the age of 10.

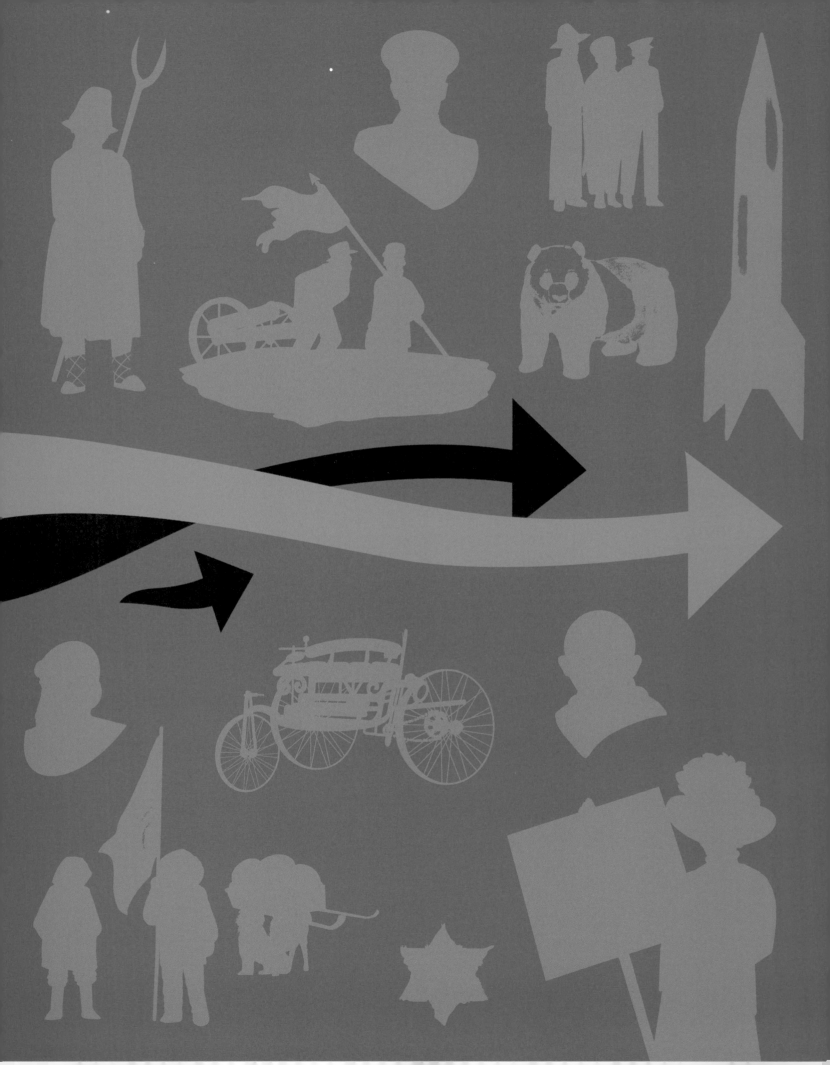

CHAPTER 5

THE WORLD AT WAR

The century between 1850 and 1950 saw the world transformed. Many things became truly global, including war and disease. Humans reached both the North and the South Poles for the first time. European invaders made further inroads into Africa and divided the continent between them. White Americans pressed farther west, driving out and abusing the Indigenous peoples. They changed the landscape, killing the herds of bison that previously roamed the plains and tearing up the prairie grass to plant farm crops.

With much of the world under European rule, when war broke out in Europe in 1914, and again in 1939, it soon escalated into World Wars that drew in people from colonies. War was a spur to developing new technology. The First World War saw tanks and planes used; the Second World War brought nuclear weapons and rocket-powered bombs—but it also brought new medicines with antibiotics, first used to treat soldiers.

THE INVASION OF AFRICA

While European powers had been active in East Asia for a long time and the British Empire controlled India, Africa was largely unexplored by Europeans. The Portuguese, British, and French had set up trading posts around the coast, but most trade was carried out with Africans who went inland bringing metals, ivory, and enslaved people to trade. As some nations banned the slave trade, colonial powers looked for other ways to make money from Africa. This would be disastrous for Africa and Africans.

A HOSTILE ENVIRONMENT

Europeans going inland to the "interior" of Africa faced problems and often died. Tropical diseases, hostile Africans defending their land and goods, and shortages of food and drink killed many. In 1876, the Belgian king Leopold II set up the **International African Association** to research the continent and find out what lay inland. The researchers found that there were rich natural resources including gold, copper, diamonds, and rubber.

The tropical disease malaria, carried by mosquitoes, killed many Europeans who went to Africa.

CARVING UP THE CONTINENT

Once Europeans knew of Africa's natural wealth, they became eager to take it. At a conference in Berlin in 1884, 12 European states, the Ottoman (Turkish) Empire, and the USA divided up the continent between them in the **Scramble for Africa**. No representatives of African nations were present. The Europeans treated Africa as available to be divided in whatever way they agreed—and then set off to claim their lands. Before the Berlin conference, 10 percent of Africa was under European rule, but by 1914 that had risen to nearly 90 percent.

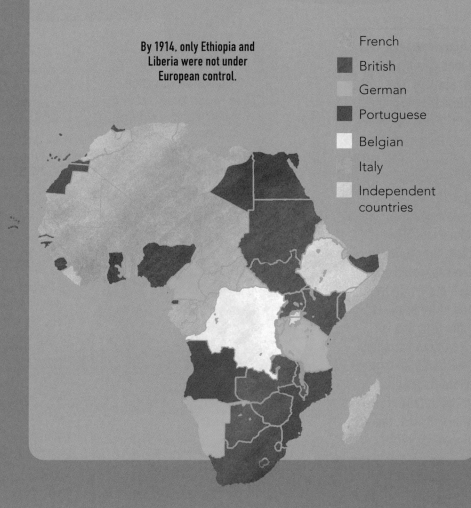

By 1914, only Ethiopia and Liberia were not under European control.

French

British

German

Portuguese

Belgian

Italy

Independent countries

DOMINATING AFRICA

The colonial powers forced their own ideas and ways of life on the people in the countries they took over. Many people were forced to speak the language of the invaders, such as English or French, and these are still official languages in many parts of Africa. European education systems and styles of government were forced on African people, and their original systems disappeared along with some of their languages. The worst impact, though, was on individuals. Many died of diseases brought in by Europeans. Many were forced to work for the invaders for low pay, were ill-treated or killed, and had their land and possessions stolen. The **Herero people** of German South West Africa (Namibia) rebelled against the German colonists taking their land and cattle. Their uprising was crushed, and the Herero people were slaughtered, or imprisoned at the Shark Island concentration camp in 1904.

Herero prisoners

WAR WITH TECHNOLOGY

Modern technology helped Europeans to take Africa. The invaders produced maps of the regions they traveled through, and laid **railroads** to gain access to the interior. The landscape of forest, mountains, and desert made travel difficult, and building railroads was the most effective way of linking the interior to the coast. Europeans built railroads in Africa in order to move troops around (to secure and maintain territories), to move mined metals, and to move crops from productive farming areas. All goods had to be transported to the coast for an onward journey by ship.

SUFFRAGE

In a democracy, the people can vote for representatives who set the laws and govern for them. Although the earliest democracy was in Greece more than 2,000 years ago, only men were allowed to vote in elections until recently. Women's battle for the vote, or for "suffrage," was a long and bitter struggle fought around the world. The latest state to allow women to vote was Saudi Arabia in 2015.

EARLY VOICES

Some people started campaigning for **women to have the vote** from the 18th century. In fact, the state of New Jersey in America granted the vote to White women who owned property in 1776—but then took it away again. In Sweden, women could vote from 1718 to 1772. Female chieftains of the Iroquois tribe in North America are recorded as being able to vote in 1654, and perhaps many other groups that have not left written records also allowed women to play a part in government. Through Europe and North America, women began to campaign vigorously in the later 1800s for the right to vote.

PROTEST AND PUNISHMENT

In some countries, particularly in Britain, there was a split between women who would go on peaceful protests and more militant campaigners who would disrupt events and damage property. Emmeline Pankhurst led the breakaway group, the Women's Social and Political Union, in 1903. They called themselves **suffragettes**, while the more law-abiding group were **suffragists**. Many of these more militant protesters were arrested and imprisoned.

NOT ALL WOMEN (OR MEN) ARE EQUAL

Today, modern democracies allow all people above a certain age to vote. In the past, before women could even vote at all, men could often only vote if they **owned property** or were of a **certain social class**. When countries such as Britain and the USA introduced votes for women, they first started with women who owned property. The voting age for women was generally older than that for men. In Australia, women who owned property could vote in local elections from 1864. When a new law was passed in 1902 allowing more women to vote in national elections, Indigenous women were excluded.

In prison, many women went on **hunger strike**, refusing to eat. They were force-fed, a cruel process that involved pushing a tube down the throat to pour food directly into the stomach. This was intended to break the woman's spirit, and often caused real physical harm. From 1913, women in danger of death from hunger strike and force-feeding were released from prison until their health recovered. Then they were taken back in, and the process continued.

EQUALITY AT LAST

In the USA, the first national march for women's suffrage took place in 1913 in Washington. Although women had been campaigning for the vote since 1848, only four states allowed women to vote in state elections, and that hadn't changed since 1896. Led by Alice Paul, American women wanted women throughout the USA to have voting rights. The **constitution was changed** in 1920, but it took decades before all women, and particularly Black women, were able to vote. In Britain, women over 30 were allowed to vote from 1918. Ten years later, the age was dropped to 21, the same as for men.

THE FIRST WORLD WAR

The First World War didn't come as a surprise. Tension had been building for a long time. The countries of Europe had made treaties (agreements) to support one another if they were attacked, and many had been growing their armies and stores of weapons. The Triple Entente (France, Russia, and Britain) were on one side, and the Triple Alliance (Germany, Austria-Hungary, and Italy) on the other. It was a tense time that took only a small trigger to plunge the continent—and then the world—into the most devastating war there had ever been.

FROM ONE DEATH TO MILLIONS

Archduke **Franz Ferdinand** was assassinated in 1914 by a Serbian group working to free Bosnia from rule by Austria-Hungary. A few days later, Austria-Hungary declared war on Serbia. Russia opposed Austria-Hungary, and the powers of the Triple Alliance and Triple Entente soon followed into the war. The Turkish Ottoman Empire joined on the side of the Triple Alliance. The war lasted until 1918, and around **20 million people died**.

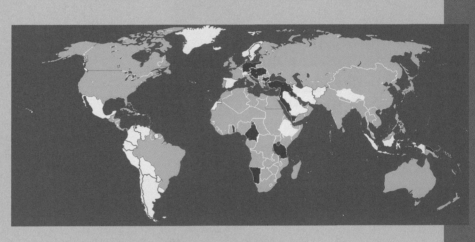

Triple Entente   ■ Triple Alliance

INTO THE TRENCHES

Germany planned first to defeat France on its western frontier, and then attack Russia. It wasn't that easy. War with France soon turned into slow battles fought from **trenches** dug through the fields of Belgium and France. Hundreds of thousands of soldiers lived and died in appalling conditions, and the surrounding countryside and villages were destroyed.

COLONIES AND BEYOND

Many European nations had **colonies** in other parts of the world, and these were **drawn into the conflict**. New Zealand (British) invaded Samoa (German), and Australia (British) attacked New Guinea (German). Japan declared war on Germany and Austria-Hungary, and attacked German ports in China. Colonies in Africa fought on the sides of their colonial overlords. The British Army in India, larger than the British army itself, fought for Britain. Battlefronts extended around Asia and Africa as well as Europe. In the seas, ships of opposing sides attacked one another. Ships and submarines also fought to stop the transport of troops and delivery of essential items, including food and weapons.

German U-boats were armed submarines that targeted military and merchant shipping

THE LAST "OLD" WAR

The First World War saw the transformation from old-style war to more **modern war**. It was the last war to have large cavalry units (soldiers on horseback) and to use cannons. It was the first war to use fighter planes, machine guns, barbed wire, and poisoned gas.

AN END TO THE "WAR TO END ALL WARS"

Countries entered and left the war. Russia withdrew after its second revolution in 1917. Romania left soon after. America entered the war as a response to German attacks on American shipping, part of Germany's plan to starve Britain by cutting off supplies. In 1918, German troops were pushed back, and it became clear they were losing. Unrest in Germany turned into revolution. In November, the kaiser (king) abdicated and the war was over in days. In 1919, the Weimar Republic was declared, with a government made up of a president, chancellor, and parliament. A **treaty** drawn up at **Versailles**, France, imposed harsh punishment on Germany, including huge compensation payments and a ban on having an army.

The German, Austro-Hungarian, Ottoman, and Russian empires all fell, borders were redrawn in Europe, new republics were founded, and some nations were re-established as independent states.

THE SECOND WORLD WAR

After the First World War and the hard times that followed, many people in Europe became nationalists—they had a fierce sense of national identity and wanted their own country to succeed. This was especially true in Germany, which suffered a great deal after the First World War. Nationalism led directly to the Second World War, which had the highest death toll of any war ever: more than 50 million people died, over half of them from the USSR.

READY FOR WAR

Hardship in Germany enabled the Nazi ("Nationalsozialismus") leader **Hitler** to rise to power. He offered the German people hope of being proud of their nation again, but their trust was misplaced. Hitler wanted to engineer a "master race" of Germans and to build an empire (or "Reich") that would last for 1,000 years. He began by persecuting Jewish people, destroying their businesses, and removing their rights. He took over Austria and part of Czechoslovakia for Germany. In 1939, he invaded part of Poland. Other European nations had put up with Hitler until this point, a policy called "appeasement," but would not tolerate him invading other European countries. Britain and France declared war on Germany. In 1940, Germany invaded France and Belgium, and despite British help, France was overcome and had to surrender.

Jewish people in areas occupied by Germany were forced to wear a special badge identifying them as Jews. This made it easy to persecute them.

WAR FROM THE AIR

The Second World War was the first major war in which **planes** were very important. Hitler planned to invade Britain and tried to defeat the British air force first with a battle in the air, but Britain won. Then German planes bombed London and other British cities in an attack known as the **Blitz**. Aerial bombing of cities remained an important strand of the war and killed thousands of civilians. British forces also fire-bombed German cities, reducing some historic cities to ashes.

During the Blitz, people living in London sheltered from the bombs in Tube (metro) stations

Bombed cities often burned for days. The fire-bombing of Dresden in Germany was a humanitarian catastrophe.

TECHNOLOGY OF WAR

Both sides raced to develop new and more powerful weapons. Germany was the first to get **rocket-powered bombs**, as rockets had already been in development before the war. Planes improved on both sides. The most devastating technology developed for the war was the **atomic bomb**, made in the USA. This harnessed atomic power for the first time, breaking atoms apart to release a devastating blast of energy.

Many women worked in ammunitions factories, making bombs

THE WORLD FIGHTS

As in the First World War, the war spread beyond Europe. European nations with empires called on their colonies for troops. Colonies were attacked and blockaded by the enemy to disrupt shipping lines bringing essential food, troops, and other supplies. Japan entered the war on the side of Germany, and attacked China and British colonies in East Asia. An attack by Japanese planes on **Pearl Harbor**, where American war ships were docked, brought the USA into the war in 1941. Disruption to shipping threatened food supplies, and people in some European countries suddenly had to grow far more of their own food.

ANNIHILATION

In his drive for racially "pure" Germans, Hitler aimed to wipe out Jewish people and other groups, including people with disabilities and Roma people. They were sent to **concentration camps** in Germany and Poland, where many were murdered immediately and others were worked to death. When the camps were opened by British and American soldiers at the end of the war, the full horror of what had happened there was revealed.

Auschwitz concentration camp

TYRANTS AND DICTATORS

The 20th century saw several oppressive, and often brutal, governments in Europe, Asia, South America, and parts of Africa. These were generally under the control of a dictator—a ruler who had seized power or extended his power beyond the level that the country's constitution (rules of government) generally allowed. When a dictator stoops to abuse of their power and commits atrocities against their own people, they become a tyrant.

LEFT AND RIGHT ALIKE

Dictators can be politically right-wing or left-wing. Although they may come from different starting points, their extreme positions often end up looking very similar: oppressing the people, using violence, secret police forces, and persecuting anyone they see as opponents. As they have absolute power, their ideas and actions aren't softened by the advice of others.

Tyrants make a lot of enemies, and many are assassinated or overthrown. Fear of this often drives them to obsessively hunt out and destroy opponents.

Tsar Ivan IV inherited power, abdicated in 1564, and returned as a tyrant with absolute power. In 1570, he had the city of Novgorod entirely destroyed.

THE ROAD TO POWER

Dictators and tyrants come to power by different routes. Some rise through military force or revolutions. Others begin by inheriting power or winning an election, but then extend their power illegally.

Tyrants of the 20th century include Stalin in the USSR, Adolf Hitler in Germany, Mao Zedong in China, Idi Amin in Uganda, Pol Pot in Cambodia, Franco in Spain, Augusto Pinochet in Chile, and Kim Jung Il in North Korea.

Stalin came to power peacefully after the death of Lenin. Like many dictators, he held **rigged elections** so that he appeared to hold power legally.

Mao Zedong was the leader of a revolutionary army that won the Chinese civil war. Pol Pot was a revolutionary who won over the peasantry of Cambodia, then attacked and defeated the unpopular government in 1974.

Stalin ruled the USSR unopposed for almost 30 years

IDEOLOGIES AND PERSONALITIES

Some dictators have powerful (though misguided) **beliefs in ideas** that direct what they do. Hitler believed in the superiority of the German people, and that Germany could and should be the greatest power in Europe. Mao Zedong and Pol Pot pushed communist ideologies, regardless of the suffering and death they caused.

Others focus on their own **desire for power**. Amin and Pinochet killed thousands whom they saw as threats to their power. Kim Il Sung, ruler of North Korea 1948–1994, built a personality cult around himself. People who did not sufficiently revere him were often killed or imprisoned. He divided citizens into "core," "wavering," or "hostile," depending on how loyal to him they were. This categorization affected all aspects of their life, including the work they could do, how much food they had, and where they could live.

Idi Amin

Kim Il Sung

An **army** can be a threat to any leader, as it has people and weapons. General Francisco Franco in Spain and General Augusto Pinochet in Chile both used armies they commanded to seize power. Franco led rebel troops in Spain's civil war in the 1930s, while Pinochet led a coup to overthrow the elected president Salvador Allende, who had appointed him general of the Chilean army. In 1971, Idi Amin overthrew the president, Milton Obote, while head of the army in Uganda.

KEEPING CONTROL

Tyrants rely on a vicious **secret police force** and encouraging people to betray each other. In Stalin's USSR, anyone suspected of opposing the communists was sent to a "gulag," a prison camp in freezing Siberia where they were kept in terrible conditions and forced to work, often to death. In Chile, Pinochet used the army to find opponents who were then imprisoned, tortured, or killed.

Political prisoners were forced to do back-breaking work despite being severely malnourished

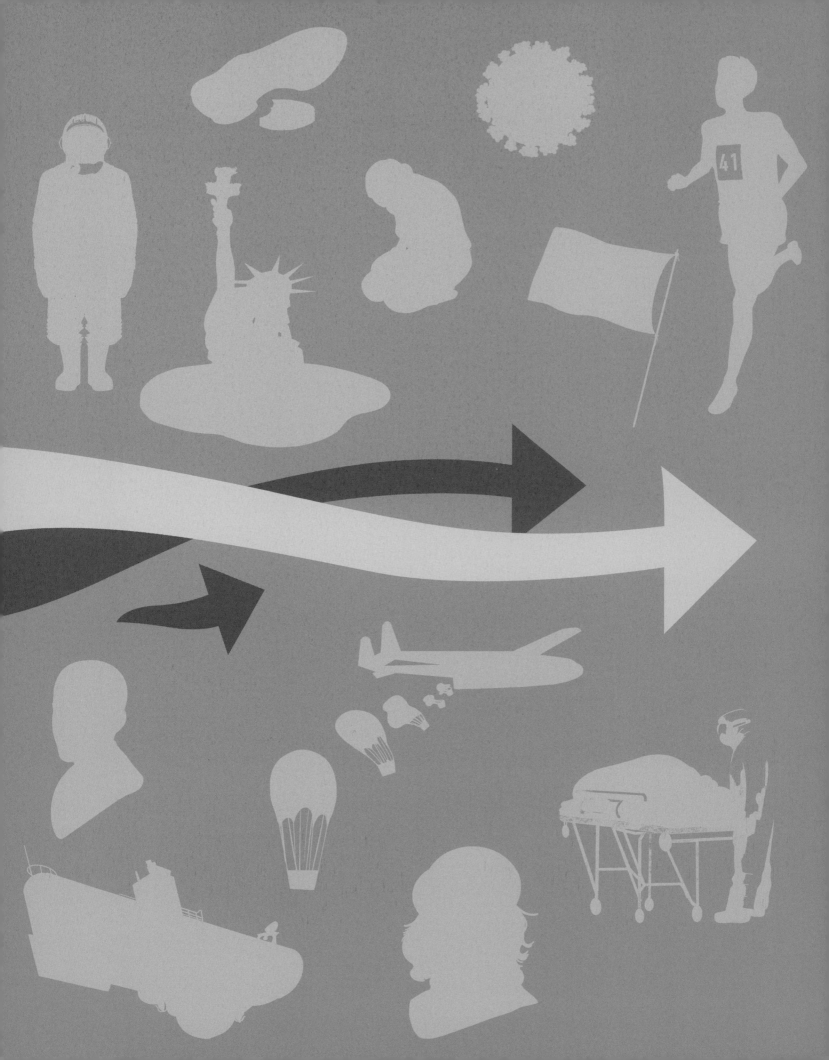

CHAPTER 6

THE MODERN WORLD

After the Second World War, the modern world began to take shape. Some countries that had become newly independent struggled to find their way at first. Many were poor, having lost their resources to colonial powers in the 18th and 19th centuries. For the second half of the 20th century, too, the world was roughly divided by the Cold War into communist and capitalist powers, each feeling threatened by the other.

The opposition between communist and western states decreased with the fall of the USSR, but new tensions emerged, particularly between some Arab Muslim countries and the west. The end of the 20th century saw a new kind of global cooperation through trade that has been called globalization.

The production of food and goods is spread around the world, and some commercial businesses have become as large and powerful as some nations. But this has brought its own problems, and nationalism—a focus on national pride rather than international cooperation—has grown in the 21st century.

1950–1964

Tension between east and west, communist and capitalist states, turned into real fighting in Vietnam and hotspots in Europe and Cuba. The USA had its own problems, stemming from the continuing mistreatment of Black people, while China suffered under Mao's rule.

1955

The **Warsaw Pact** was a defence treaty between the Soviet Union and seven other communist states in central and eastern Europe: Albania, Bulgaria, Czechoslovakia, East Germany, Hungary, Poland, and Romania. It was signed after (then) West Germany joined the western NATO alliance, to try to balance NATO power.

1950

The USSR and the People's Republic of China (PRC) sign a Treaty of Friendship, Alliance, and Mutual Assistance. Several governments around the world, including the UK government, officially **recognize the PRC**.

1954

The British athlete Roger Bannister became the first person to **run a mile (1.6 km) in under four minutes**.

1955–1975

The **Vietnam War** raged between communist North Vietnam and South Vietnam. South Vietnam was supported by the USA with its policy to fight communism anywhere it arose. The war was long and difficult, with many atrocities committed against civilians (non-soldiers). It became increasingly unpopular in the USA, and they withdrew from it in 1973. The war ended in 1976, with Vietnam unified as the Socialist Republic of Vietnam.

1950

1953

The mountaineers Edmund Hillary from New Zealand and Tenzing Norgay from Nepal became the first people to climb **Mount Everest**, the highest mountain in the world.

1955–1968

The fight for equality by Black people in the USA began as a grassroots movement after a Black woman, **Rosa Parks**, was arrested for refusing to give up her seat in a White-only section of a bus.

The civil rights movement fought for the rights of Black American citizens. In the 1950s, Black people often had to use different facilities from White people, and had fewer rights. They couldn't travel on the same buses, use the same schools, or often even live in the same areas. The civil rights movement used both violent and peaceful protests as it campaigned for equal and fair treatment.

1957

The first satellite, **Sputnik 1**, was launched into space by the USSR, starting the "space race" between the USSR and USA (see pages 116–117).

Sputnik 1, just 56 cm (22 in) across, sent simple radio signals to Earth for several weeks

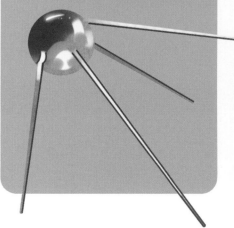

1958–1962

Mao Zedong introduced the **Great Leap Forward**, a policy intended to modernize China's industry and agriculture and solidify Chinese communism. It was a terrible failure, leading to the deadliest famine in history, killing 15–55 million people in 1959–1961.

The Trieste was crewed by Don Walsh and Jacques Piccard.

1960s–1994

In South Africa, 3.5 million Black people were forcibly removed from their land into areas known as **Bantu homelands**, where they were plunged into poverty. Their farms were sold cheaply to White farmers.

1960

The first crewed vehicle reached the bottom of the **Mariana Trench** in the Pacific Ocean, the deepest part of Earth's seas, at 11 km (7 miles) deep.

1962

The **Cuban Missile Crisis** brought Earth close to full-scale nuclear war (see page 113).

1964

1959

Revolutionaries **Che Guevara** and **Fidel Castro** overthrew the government of Cuba. The previous government, led by General Batista, had the support of the USA. The new government began a nationalization programme, and the USA responded with a trade embargo (a refusal to do trade). Cuba then appealed, successfully, to the USSR for support.

1960

The **Valdivia earthquake** in Chile was the most powerful ever recorded.

1961

Russian cosmonaut Yuri Gagarin became the **first human in space** in a small space capsule called Vostok 1.

THE COLD WAR

Although Britain, France, and the USA had fought alongside the USSR in the Second World War, they trusted each other less and less in the following years. This led to the Cold War, a time of open hostility between them. At times, the Cold War was in danger of turning into a real—and probably nuclear—war. It ended in 1991 with the collapse of the USSR.

COMMUNISM VERSUS CAPITALISM

At the heart of the Cold War was a **conflict of ideology**. The communists supported a strong central government and communal ownership of land, factories, and public goods. The Communist Party was always in power, and there were no democratic elections. Communist societies were heavily policed, with brutal punishments for anyone who opposed the state. The western capitalist countries supported personal and economic freedom. People chose their government in democratic elections, and were generally free to discuss politics without fear of a secret police force. Private ownership of businesses, land, and public goods produced both opportunity and social inequality.

Each side distrusted the other, and spying was big business. This shoe has a hidden radio transmitter for a spy to use to send messages secretly.

The conflict between east and west was played out on the world stage. In 1950, communist North Korea invaded South Korea in the hope of unifying the country. South Korea resisted, and the USA entered the war to defend South Korea against attack by the communists. It was the first armed conflict of the Cold War.

BLOCKING BERLIN

After the Second World War, **Europe split into east and west**, with the east under communist rule. Germany was split into East and West parts and the capital city, Berlin, was also split into East and West, although it was in the area controlled by the USSR. Stalin worried that the west would try to seize East Germany. In 1948, he cut all land routes into West Berlin, starting a blockade that lasted 11 months. West Berlin soon ran short of food, medicines, fuel, and other essentials. The allies (Britain, France, and the USA) air-dropped supplies to West Berlin until Stalin lifted the blockade in 1949. The Berlin blockade was the start of the Cold War.

Essential supplies were dropped by planes into West Berlin

EUROPE DIVIDED

Fiercely guarded borders divided east and west Europe, and citizens of the east weren't allowed to move to the west. The division of east and west became most visible in 1961, when the USSR ordered the East German communist government to build the **Berlin Wall**, separating East and West Berlin. The Wall cruelly divided friends and family, since East Germans weren't allowed to cross it.

People peered through gaps in the Berlin Wall to see friends on the other side—or just to see what was going on

Nuclear bunkers, hidden behind huge metal doors, were vast underground living spaces with supplies for many people

WAITING FOR WAR

East and west both stockpiled weapons and raced to produce more and more powerful bombs. Both sides tried out their deadly atomic weapons in tests, displaying their strength. They built **nuclear bunkers** where people could shelter if nuclear war happened. Much of this was just for show: Nuclear war between the two superpowers would have devastated the world, and nuclear bunkers would have been of little use.

TIPPING POINT

The most critical moment of the Cold War came in 1961. The USA tried to prompt an uprising against the communists in Fidel Castro's Cuba, but failed. In response, the USSR moved **nuclear missiles to Cuba**, aimed at the USA. After a tense few days of negotiation in 1962, the USSR agreed to remove its missiles, and the USA agreed to remove its own missiles from Turkey. War was narrowly avoided.

THE SPACE RACE

The Cold War wasn't only about spying, military hostility, and disliking the other side's politics. There was competition in all areas, including sports, technology, and space exploration. The "space race" was the race between the USSR and the USA to get into space. The USSR was in the lead at first, but the USA claimed victory by putting humans on the Moon in 1969.

OFF THE GROUND

The first **rockets** were made in Germany in the 1920s. They were soon adapted as bombs in the Second World War, and their use as spacecraft was put on hold until later. In 1947, scientists in America sent fruit flies and seeds into space to test the effect of cosmic rays on them, and during the 1940s and 50s both the USA and USSR sent unfortunate monkeys, mice, and dogs into space, most of which died. These rocket trips were up and then down, just entering space and returning, but in 1957 the USSR used a rocket to launch the first satellite, Sputnik. It stayed in orbit for several weeks.

THE MOON AND BEYOND

The American president, J.F. Kennedy, was determined that America should not fall behind in the space race. In 1961, he announced that Americans would **land on the Moon** before the end of the decade. The American Apollo program first sent spacecraft to the Moon with no crew, then took humans around the Moon, and finally landed in July 1969.

A huge rocket launched each Apollo craft, but only a tiny top portion traveled to the Moon

PEOPLE IN SPACE

The USSR was first to get a **man into space** (Yuri Gagarin in 1961) and then a **woman** (Valentina Tereshkova in 1963). Indeed, although American Alan Shepard visited space in 1961, it took more than 20 years for an American woman to follow—Sally Ride in 1983. In 1965, the USSR achieved another first when Alexei Leonov left his craft and floated in space for 12 minutes—called a "space walk."

Valentina Tereshkova

By sending humans and robots into space and building space stations, we have found out much more about the universe

Lunokhod 1 rover

Voskhod 2 spacecraft

Luna 1 orbiter

Salyut 1 space station

Venera 4 was a probe sent to explore Venus

While reaching the Moon was a major focus, it wasn't the only aim of the space race. Soviet craft were sent to **Venus** and **Mars**, but with a high failure rate. The first "soft" (non-crash) landing on Venus was in 1970. The Soviet Venera craft were the first to enter the atmosphere of another planet, the first to land successfully on another planet, and the first to record sounds on another planet. The first Soviet landing on Mars in 1971 was only briefly successful. The USA had more success; in 1965, Mariner 4 sent back the first close-up photos of the Martian surface.

AT HOME IN SPACE

Both the USA and the USSR wanted a permanent base in space, and both set out to build **space stations**. The first success was the USSR's Salyut station, which started operating in 1971. The first US space station, Skylab, was operational from 1973. On a space station, astronauts can carry out experiments and conduct space walks using a suitable spacesuit.

The space race ended in 1975 when astronauts from the USSR and USA met in space. An Apollo and a Soyuz spacecraft docked in space and the two commanders, Thomas Stafford and Alexei Leonov, shook hands.

USA

USSR

117

COVID-19

The worldwide pandemic of COVID-19 (the short name for Coronavirus Disease 2019) that began in 2020 was the worst since the flu of 1918–1919 (see page 97). In May 2023, The World Health Organization (WHO) said there had been nearly 766 million confirmed cases and 7 million deaths globally. First detected in China, it quickly spread around the world. Attempts to stop its spread came too late and were soon abandoned. Most nations then focused on slowing its spread, hoping to prevent health services being overwhelmed, and to buy time for a vaccine to be developed.

A NEW DISEASE

The first cases of a new **respiratory disease** emerged in China in late 2019. Caused by a **virus** carried in micro-aerosols (tiny particles that can stay airborne for a long time) in the air and large droplets on hands and surfaces, COVID-19 attacks people's lungs, causing coughing, fever, and other symptoms. It probably crossed to humans from pangolins or bats in or near a Chinese food market, or possibly came from a research laboratory, though we don't know for sure. The death rate from COVID-19 was high at first, particularly among older people and those who were already unwell in other ways, and were less able to fight the disease. Because people continued to travel when it first emerged, the virus spread quickly around the world and soon became a global pandemic.

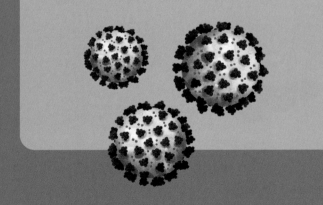

A WORLD CLOSED DOWN

Some countries closed their borders to foreign travel, but the disease had already taken hold and could only be slowed, not stopped. Many nations introduced **restrictions** forcing people to stay at home, to keep a safe distance from others, and to wear protective face masks when outside their homes. Movement was restricted: Schools, workplaces, and shops were closed, and gatherings of people were banned.

Cities were eerily empty, as people were not allowed outside without a good reason

CRISIS IN CARE

In many countries, **hospitals could not cope** with the number of COVID patients needing care. Some ran out of oxygen and other vital supplies. Doctors and nurses also caught COVID, so there were fewer staff working in hospitals. In some places, such as China, new hospitals were built very quickly to provide more beds for people sick with COVID. In other places, people were looked after at home without specialist care.

Many people taken to hospital survived on ventilators, but others died

RACE FOR A VACCINE

Scientists immediately began trying to make a **vaccine** to prevent people developing serious symptoms from COVID-19. The first vaccines began to be used in late 2020. In many places, they were offered first to healthcare workers and the most vulnerable people. The vaccines offered some protection against getting COVID, but were most valuable in preventing serious illness or death in people who did catch it. By early 2023, an estimated 70 percent of the world's population had received at least one vaccination against COVID.

TRUTH AND ANTI-TRUTH

Many **conspiracy theories** grew up around COVID-19. Some people claimed either that the disease had been created in a laboratory and released deliberately or accidentally, or that the pandemic was a hoax and there was no such disease.

This highlighted the issues we have in the modern world with working out what is truth and what is not. With so many sources of information available, it can be difficult to find out what is really going on, especially since sometimes we are told "fake news" by people who want to influence us in some way. The emergence of AI technology is making this problem even more complicated, as well as raising many other questions.

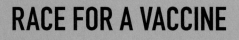

NO TO MANDATORY VACCINES!

Some people objected to mandatory (when you have to do something) vaccines, to wearing a face mask, and to other measures designed to slow the spread of COVID-19

FUTURE HISTORY

History doesn't just stop. Events are continuously happening that will later become history. These could be negative, such as global pandemics, wars, economic or political troubles, or natural disasters, or positive, such as scientific breakthroughs, increased international cooperation, or just everyday acts of kindness that change the world for the better. For now, you are living in the future's history.

CLIMATE IN CRISIS

People have known since the 1800s that increasing the amount of carbon dioxide in Earth's atmosphere could warm the planet. The evidence for **climate change** happening was clear by the late 20th century, but governments have been slow to take meaningful action. Already, higher average temperatures are causing more extreme weather events, droughts, floods, wildfires, crop failure, and melting ice. As temperatures rise worldwide, the areas we can live in comfortably will change, and people will have to move around or change how they live.

Melting ice at the Poles and in glaciers threatens to drown coastal cities

Hot and dry air makes wildfires more likely

Drought makes it hard to farm crops and animals

RUNNING OUT

Earth has **limited supplies** of the things we need and use. Some of these are running out. To preserve valuable resources, we can reduce waste and recycle more. But people are also looking at new places to find some of the metals we need—under the ice, on the seabed, and even in outer space. One plan is to capture **asteroids** in space and mine them for the metals we need for our lifestyles. Future historians will know whether or not this becomes workable.

Will asteroids become the source of materials for our future phones and other items?

BEYOND EARTH

Humankind's voyage into **space** has only just begun. A crewed mission to Mars is likely in the near future, and at some point we will probably build bases on the Moon or Mars, or elsewhere. Some people believe humans will colonize other planets, but this would be a long way in the future. It's sometimes suggested as a solution to coping with worsening conditions on Earth. One day, our lives might be part of humankind's early Earth history while people have spread far and wide through space!

CONNECTED OR DISCONNECTED?

International problems in the 21st century have shown that in a connected world, everyone is threatened when things go wrong. Most countries depend on others for supplies— whether of food, fuel, or consumer goods. Disruption spreads far beyond one country's borders. The Russian invasion of Ukraine in 2022 caused global problems with food and fuel supplies. Rising nationalism has also led to some countries distancing themselves from others, hoping to protect their trade and borders with isolationist policies including a limit to immigration. The UK left the European trading bloc in 2021.

Many countries have ageing populations and need more workers, while others face war, climate change, and other problems that drive people overseas. These challenges seem to need **cooperation** to solve. Will the world become more or less connected in the future? Both have advantages and disadvantages.

LOOKING AHEAD

There are lots of problems in the world, but it's important to remember that humankind has faced very tough challenges before and survived. If we **pay attention to history**, we can learn lessons from the past and use them to help us take positive action in the present. One day, future historians will look back on the steps we took to address the issues facing us now and use that knowledge to help them with their own problems. Let's make our story one worth remembering!

Future historians might live in sustainable green cities

INDEX